Praise for Adam Jameson:

"In Adam Jameson's new work, Monks Love the Curve Ball, this Kansas-seer, native son explores the rhythmic and sometimes eccentric serenity of everyday life in his part of the world. We welcome in his life of baseball games, both past and present, earth tilling, splitting wood: *Splitting wood by hand tends to keep the people away,* useful workadays, writing, duck hunting and good dogs. To say baseball is just a metaphor for things like ritual, community and family is almost a disservice. He's occupying the terrain somewhere between Wendell Berry's farmer/poet and Jack Spicer's baseball afficionado/poet, who once wrote: *The pitcher, in his sudden humanness, looks toward the dugout in either agony or triumph.* Adam's triumph is his language: plain-spoken, passionate and revealing."

-John Macker, Author of *The Blues Drink Your Dreams Away* and *Atlas of Wolves.*

More praise for Adam Jameson:

"Jameson's poems make the ordinary sacred. *Monks Love the Curveball* celebrates his passionate love of family, baseball, work and hunting. Lyrical and objective, the poems are snapshots of the moment, while celebrating the passage of time. I feel more human, more alive after reading these poems because as a father and former baseball player his vision is universal, a vision I can feel in my bones."

-John Knoll, *Ghosting America*

MONKS LOVE THE CURVEBALL

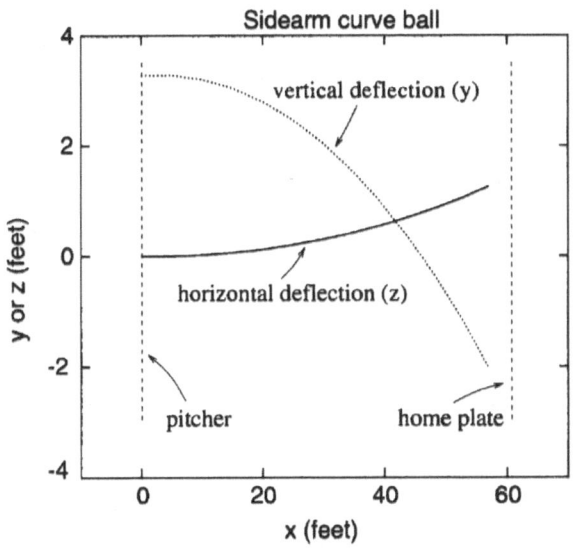

POEMS BY ADAM JAMESON

Kansas City — Missouri

Spartan Press
Kansas City, MO
spartanpresskc.com

Copyright © Adam Jameson, 2020
First Edition1 3 5 7 9 10 8 6 4 2
ISBN: 978-1-950380-92-3
LCCN: 2020932158

Design, edits and layout: Jason Ryberg
Author photo: Meredith Jameson
All rights reserved. No part of this publication may be reproduced or transmitted in any form or by any means, electronic or mechanical, including photocopying, recording or by info retrieval system, without prior written permission from the author.

Acknowledgements:

The author wishes to thank the editors of the following journals in which some of these poems have previously appeared.

Harp, Bards Against Hunger, The Little Balkans Review, To the Stars through Difficulty, 39 West Press and Spartan Press, The Writer's Almanac with Garrison Keillor.

TABLE OF CONTENTS

Major

That's What Happens When you Leave
   a Fastball Pecker High / 1
Splitting Wood on Robert Bly's Birthday-Ghost Sign / 2
Frank Ferraro-Ghost Sign / 3
Major / 4
Staking on 680th / 5
Windstorm-Ghost Sign / 7
Talking With Uncle Trout / 8
Shaman / 10
Monks Love the Curveball / 11

Southpaw Catcher

Christmas Present / 15
Watering the Oaks-Ghost sign / 16
Southpaw Catcher-Ghost Sign / 18
3 miles of Line/Lab Love / 20
Rest Period / 22
Catching a Lefty / 23
Thunderstorm / 24
Saturday-Ghost Sign / 25
Super Bowl Sunday / 27
Don't Bother Men While They Are Working / 28
Summer-Ghost Sign / 30

Fall Day-Ghost Sign / 31

Pitching / 33

Beaver Lake-Ghost Sign / 34

Sleet Storm / 35

Middle Age

Night Before Series / 39

Middle Age / 40

Dispatcher / 42

Hasn't Thrown a Straight Ball Yet / 43

Acceptance / 44

Wild Red Berry Field-Ghost Sign / 45

Double Play / 47

Cashero to Cole / 48

188 Pitches / 50

That Damn 7 Switch / 51

I dedicated my 1st book to my wife Meredith, my son Cole and my sister Julie. I also included my Mom Sheryl who passed away far to soon at age 50. This book is also for them because I'm not the man I am without them, but I also need to include the people and places of Southeast Kansas, aka the *Little Balkans*. Like my wife, son and Mom the people and places of the Balkans have made me who I am today.

Foreword – Monks Love the Curveball

Adam Jameson didn't invent first person, narrative poetry but he certainly has his own way of transforming it into both observation and participation.

It's automatic writing in a voice that does not force the reader to unravel the poem but rather quietly offers it up as is, without concealment. As in this one, titled Windstorm.

> *I found Underwood and*
> *the crew 12 miles west*
> *of Humboldt just after 2 am.*
>
> *I brought them a transformer*
> *and a couple of cold pizzas.*
>
> *We ate by headlight*
> *in the middle of the road,*
> *wind singing through the weeds.*

I carry this poem around with me the way I carry old pictures of family and friends in my wallet. Indeed, many times, as I read through the rest of the poems in this collection, I felt as if I was leafing through black and white snapshots in a well-worn family album pulled down from the top shelf of a closet.

You too might have the same kind of Kodak experience as you read them. Or you might find yourself watching old 8 mm home movies projected by a Bell & Howell. Whichever, Adam Jameson is somewhere in each.

As I write this, the 2020 presidential election approaches and America is askew with politicians, talking heads, Facebook friends and Twitter posts filling every tiny space with what is, in my opinion, mostly self-important, living-color drivel.

One way to bring things back into alignment is poetry. So, dear reader, should you feel a little off the bubble, I invite you to shut down (or at least pause) your TV, computer and cell phone, open *Monks Love the Curveball*, and leaf through its poems for a leveling look at the world through the eyes of Adam Jameson.

J.T. Knoll
March 12, 2020
Pittsburg, Kansas

Major

That's What Happens When You Leave a Fastball Pecker High

It's been sleeting all day.
I've got a fire roaring.

Cold Dos Equis in hand.

Watching College Baseball
with my son.
He's an undersized Lefty.

I'm half asleep when
I hear the ping of ball
off aluminum bat.

I look up to see the
ball leave the park.
On his way to take
a piss he says that's
what happens when
you leave a fastball pecker high.

Major

I started hunting ducks
with my dad in the late 70's.
Never had a dog.

In 87 my single Mom
paid a grand for a
yellow lab out of Idaho.

He kept me out of jail
in high school and college.
That dog would do
anything for me.

I would have killed for him.

Late one January evening
I wounded a mallard drake.
I called and called but
he wouldn't come in.

I could see him going under
in the twilight.
In the dark I heard him slosh
through the ice up the
bank with that duck.

Staking on 680th

Staking a new pole line
with a lab and blue heeler
as company.

I rub their ears
and feed them a
couple of cookies
from my lunch pail.

Back at the truck I give
them some more cookies
before I drive off with
my tires covered in dog piss.

Splitting Wood on Robert Bly's Birthday

First day of winter vacation.
Bored by 9:30 I headed
for the shop and grandpa's
wedge maul and axe.

Mrs. Mitchell's son had
cut down a big ash in the fall.
I cut it up after 6 weeks
of no show from the son.

It was still piled on my
back property line.
I didn't need the wood.

Already had 4 cords stacked
under the pines to the north.
What I did need was some silence.

Splitting wood by hand
tends to keep the people away.

I spilt till twilight.
The only sounds were
me cussing under my breath
and the sharp rap of grandpa's
maul hitting the wedge.

Frank Ferraro

After a game he used
to pile Denny and I
in the back of his Cadillac.

Covered in dirt and chalk,
we'd sink into the deep
leather and let the AC
cool our sweat.

He and Dee would talk
over the game as we
cruised south, headed
for burgers and Coke's.

Denny and I would order
a couple of cheeseburgers
and fries.

Frank would open his
wallet with his thick
plumber's fingers, fish
in among the hundreds
and come out with a 20.

He'd always tell the girl
behind the counter to get
us another burger or two.
These are growing boys.

After a hard fought
victory this summer
I took my team to the
Sno-Cone stand.

Two of my favorites
asked for a 2nd cone.
Smiling, I handed the
girl a 20 and said better
get these boys a couple of more.

Windstorm

I found Underwood and
the crew 12 miles west
of Humboldt just after 2 am.

I brought them a transformer
and a couple of cold pizzas.

We ate by headlight
in the middle of the road,
wind singing through the weeds.

Talking with Uncle Trout

Charlie Hough threw
butterfly knuckle balls
in the bigs until his mid-40's.

If hitters like George Brett
can't put bat on knuckle ball
then nobody can predict
the moment to moment
flight pattern of a butterfly.

The balls and ball players are juiced.
The strip pits for the most part
have become the province of the rich.

He's aged out of me coaching him.
I miss it sometimes.
Specially at Jaycee.

Me standing in the 3rd base
coaches' box and him
down in the count.

Behind a run or two.
Maybe tied.

He steps out and looks
down kind of longingly.
He never needed signs.

I'd tell him head on it or
knob back at the pitcher.

He swung a wood bat
for years. I'd close my eyes
and wait
for the crack of solid line drive.

Open my eyes to see
white ball rip through
the night. The moths
dancing around the light.

Shaman

A middle-aged Shaman
hunts ducks with his son.

2 drakes and a hen
wobble sideways
into the decoys.

He's a Lefty shooting
right handed.

He passes on the hen
and drops the 2 drakes.

A coyote lopes lazily
through the beans to the west.

Monks Love the Curveball
Benedictine College - St. Benedict's Abbey, Atchison, KS

Bases loaded.
We need the 3rd out.
They call in the lefty from right field.

Cole passes on the mandatory
warm up pitches.
He doesn't throw hard enough
to break glass but he has his
Dad's middle linebacker mind.

He sneaks 2 fastballs by on
the outside corner.
Strike 3 is a curveball that
starts middle of the plate
and winds up in the dirt.

Moms and Dads are
hoopin and hollerin.
I'm looking at the Abbey
knowing the monks
love a good curveball.

Southpaw Catcher

Christmas Present

A newly pinned RN with
a baby due on Christmas
wants a 6-pole extension
to serve her new home by the 24th.

That's a 6-week process
I tell her.
    Gotta draw plans.
    Gather material.
    Approvals.

Rough old foreman
plugged her meter in today.
Came back to the shop
with a smile under his beard.

Watering the Oaks

Twilight on Sunday evening.
Yoger's cutting wheat on
the 80 across the road.

He's throw's me a
a quick wave from the cab
before spinning the combine
to make another pass.
I used to take him chunks
of flathead every October.

I don't have time to
get to the river anymore.
He must make do with
crappie in April.

Cole and I are working
on his changeup.
Scooter is asleep in the grass.

It has been dry of late.
My wife is watering the
3 towering oaks on the
west side of the house.

I don't dare tell her
my Uncle planted
those oaks in 1953.
They don't need watered.

I crouch for one
more change up
and watch her
water the oaks.

Southpaw Catcher

At the tryouts the coach
told me that no left hander
would ever play catcher for him.

I just shrugged my shoulders
and walked back to sit
with the other parents.

2 games in and 17 passed
balls later he finally
let Cole put the gear on.

We were on our 4th pitcher.
My wife glanced at me
when she heard the click
of the pitch counter.
We got run ruled in 4 innings.

I waited till everyone had left.
Showed the coach the counter.
It read 28.
The number of pitches in the
dirt that game.

I made a *0* with my fingers
and told him that was how
many went to the backstop.

I had 12-year-old lefty
with a fat lip, 2 deep
bruises and a missing fingernail,
laughing at his dirty face in
the truck mirror.

3 Mile of Line/Lab Love

I spent the day staking
3 miles of line near Englevale.
Old coal camp played out
long ago.

Willie from Rural Water #5
locked his brakes up when
he saw me in the ditch.
Bits of gravel rained down
on my hard hat as I choked
down the dust.

Ain't got no tracer
wire on the pipe up here.
Call me when the crew
punches'er and I'll fix it.

2 poles later I watched
a doe and 2 fawns eating
beans at the edge of the field.
Far off to the south I could
hear the BNSF whistling
the crossings in Girard.

John Tersinar's 2 fat labs
heard me hammering stakes.
They came trotting down
the middle of 680th in
search of treats.

I gave them half my
sandwich,2 butternut
cookies and a thanks
for slobbering on my boots.

Rest Period

I pulled into Bo's 1 Stop
at 6:07 am.
Went to the beer cooler
and grabbed a six pack.

Stopped in the candy isle
to grab a Snickers.
Breakfast of Champions
I told the cashier.

She gave me a sideways
glance and handed me
my change.

I live a mile from Bo's.
By the time I pulled
in my drive I'd eaten
the Snickers and thrown
2 empties out the window.

Catching a Lefty

I squat behind the plate.
Cole spits sunflower seeds
in the dirt at Bill Russell field.

Catching a Lefty is hard.
Sometimes his ball moves
down and in.

Other times it's up and out.
Sometimes I got no fucking
idea where its headed.

30 pitches in he asks
if I need a break.
I sure as hell do, but
not about to tell him that.

Thunderstorm

Tonya and I slide
west toward Independence
after the storm.

She chatters away
about her daughter, her divorce,
and anything else she can think of.
I'm listening and watching
the ditches for deer.

Service operator couldn't
tell us how many outages
we had. At the building
only 2 trucks were out.

It should have been
a quick trip.
8 hour later we loaded
up and headed back east.

She chattered for a few miles
and then went silent.

I glanced over and she was asleep.

I turned down the radio
and went back to watching
the ditches for deer.

Saturday

Sitting on the sunshine
of Saturday afternoon
drinking beer and writing.

My son rides his bike with
the other kids all over
the campground.

Scooter the Shi-tzu is asleep in the sun.
Wife reads a book in the lounge chair.

Trees in half bloom.
Crappie are biting.

Camper windows open,
letting the Kansas spring
flow through, and cover
our pillows.

The deer sneak up at dusk
to eat acorns just outside
the firelight.

Only I can see them.
Everyone else is busy
talking about nothing.

I say a prayer of gratitude
between bites of crappie
and sips of beer as the
bull bats sweep low over
the water gathering
the supper
in silence.

Super Bowl Sunday

Cole and I have pitching practice
in the back yard on Super Bowl Sunday.

I dig out my mask from 30 years ago.
I can't really see the ball anymore
but can hear the seams spinning through the twilight.

Don't Bother Men While They Are Working

Crew ran short of top ties.
Called and wanted me to run
some up to just south of Hepler.

They were setting up on a pole.
I pulled off on 690th a hundred feet away.

George, one of the local KDOT guys
showed up, parked behind me.
He wanted to know if he could
have all the old poles.

Lives about a mile away on 700th.
We could set them off in his drive.

Told him I'd ask the foreman when I got the chance.

He hung around for about
10 minutes, shooting the
shit before he got antsy.

Why don't you go ask the foreman now?
They are just standing around talking.

They aren't just standing around
and talking George.
That's called a tailgate.

The foreman and crew are covering
every possible scenario they
can think of.
He's got 2 journeymen over
there under the age of 25.

Hot work. 7200 volts in the wire.
If anything goes wrong that foreman
could get somebody hurt or killed.

That foreman would have to answer
to the families, to the company
and to himself for that.

How long will it
take before they are
done with that pole?
About 45 minutes George.

I can't wait that long.
You want those poles George?
Yep. Sure do.
You run along.

I'll wait, because I'm
not about to bother
men while they are working.

Summer

I've mowed and weed whacked an acre.
Cut up the top of an old elm
that blew down in the storm last week.

Took my son and nieces
to town for ice cream.

Checked the tomato plants
and gave the neighbor's
dog some belly rubbing.

It's twilight.
I'm sitting on the deck
drinking my supper again
and watching the wrens
bed down in the bird house to the west.

Fall Day

Got up before dawn
and made coffee in
the dark kitchen.
My phone vibrated and buzzed.

Email…we had trouble
on Mulberry 23-4 last night.
I shut it off and stuck it
in the drawer by the coffee pot.

On the deck, the eastern sky
pinkish and purple, I see
Mr. Socks the cat nosing
around in my garden.
A doe and fawn eating acorns
in Mrs. Mitchell's yard.

3 teal buzz overhead, make
a hard right and land
on Stefanoni's pond.
Mr. Russian shuffles out
his driveway to get his paper.

I spent the week taking
care of linemen, troubleshooters,
mechanics, designers and supervisors
from Pittsburg to Wichita.

I really should take a look
at that Mulberry circuit, but
I'm going to rake leaves, cut
wood and leave that phone
in the drawer till Monday.

Pitching

Cole wanted to pitch today.
I swore off catching him a year ago.

We drug the mound out
and I measured off 60' 6".
I swallowed the last of my Dos Equis
and pride and sat down on my bucket.

The 1st curveball hit me square in the mask.
He choked back laughter while I
contemplated a concussion.

30 pitches in I had to bow out.
I couldn't feel my hand anymore.

He's taking a nap on the couch.
I'm in the other room wondering
if Mom was laughing at me too.

Beaver Lake

Twilight at the lake.
Cole goes for one last bike ride.

The Jackson's recently retired.
This is their 1st trip with
the camper and the boat.

I help him back it down the ramp
and quietly ask God to bless
them as they head out
in search of channel cat.

I'm back in my chair.
Cold beer in my hand, watching
fireflies turn circles just
outside the firelight.

Sleet Storm

We'd been out in the storm for an hour.
I noticed him shivering a time or two.

When I asked if he wanted to go home
all I got was a headshake no.
I didn't tell him I was freezing
my ass off, too.

We sat there in the blind
not saying a word.
Sleet was collecting on the decoys
and the brim of my hat.

Just before shooting hours were over
I saw 2 drakes coming hard.

Take 'em I whispered.

Cole dropped the 2 drakes
and I hadn't even raised my gun.

Why didn't you shoot dad?

I started to tell him about being
middle-aged, not being able to
see so good and slowing reflexes.

Instead I wiped the sleet off my face
and headed to the kayak to
pick up his birds.

Middle Age

Middle Age

I hit grounders with
an old school fungo bat.

The empty swish of the bat
mixes with twilight
and boys when I swing and miss.

Night Before the Series

I'm on the deck listening
to the radio replay of
Game 7 from 1985.

Grandpa never missed a game.
He could be found on the breezeway
of his house over in East Town whenever
the Royals were on.

Grandkids birthdays, Easter,
wedding anniversaries, you
name it, all had to be planned
around the Royals on radio.

In the spring it was work pants
and a jacket, summer was the same
work pants and undershirt, fall
was back to the jacket.
It was my job to sit quietly
on the chaise lounge and fetch
Budweiser from the fridge.

If the game ran late or the
weather was bad, Grandma
would stick her head out the door.

He would dismiss her with a
grunt and a wave of his hand.

It's where I heard Denny Matthews
talk about the speed of Wilson, the
slick fielding of White, Brett with
another double off the wall, and
the Quis coming to slam the door
in the 9th.

I'm 43 and can still see
them in my mind
all these years later.

So when this run started with
the wildcard game against
the A's, I turned off my TV,
took my son out on the
deck to listen on the radio.

When it got late, my wife
stuck her head out the door
and saw me sitting there with
a cold Bud and a 12-year-old
sound asleep in the lawn chair.

Acceptance

The crew was a man down.
Foreman asked if I could fill in
as a flagman while they changed
a pole out on the highway.

No big deal.
Hold the sign and wave
traffic through now and then.

I could tell he wasn't going to stop.
I hollered for the crew to get clear.

As he sped by, I beat his truck
with my sign and called him
every name in the book.

A little while later foreman
headed to town for drinks for the crew.
He asked if I wanted anything.

Dr. Pepper I said while I fished
in my pocket. Foreman smiled and drove off
before I could hand him my money.

Wild Red Berry Field

Piccini on the mound.
Jameson behind the plate.

They are 12.
I'm letting them call their own game.

30 years ago, I was catching another
Piccini, and calling our own game.

The count was 1 and 2.
Runner on 2nd.

2 dads' sitting on buckets
in the dugout door watch
a changeup spin towards
home plate.

Jameson squeezes the foul tip
as Piccini pumps his fist.

Dispatcher

The wind swirls out of
the south, then the north.

Giant thunderheads
begin to build on
the Colorado line.

By 3am I'll be sending
a crew to Euclid street
to turn Mrs. Elliot's lights on
and rescue her cat from
the tree.

Hasn't Thrown a Straight Ball Yet

He picked up his
radar gun while
Cole was warming up.
He put it down
after 2 pitches.

After 2 weak ground balls
and a strike out, he opened
his note pad and scribbled something.

In the next inning after another
weak ground ball
and a fly out, he scribbled some more.

He asked me which
team I was watching.

The kids in red I told him.

He and I talked a little
over the next 2 innings
about the weather and who
was the greatest hitter to ever play.

With 2 outs in the bottom
of the 7th he said that kid

on the mound hasn't thrown
a straight ball yet.
He scribbled some more.

Cole had worked 4 innings.
1 earned run. No walks. 3 strikeouts.

When he got up to leave,
The scout noticed my fat lip and small
shiner under my right eye. He asked
what in the hell happened?
I said you outta try catching
a kid who hasn't thrown a
straight ball yet.

Double Play

Weak grounder to 3rd.
Runner on 3rd   waits for
the throw to 1st.

O'Hara fires a dart to 1st.

The dugout screams 4!
Dawson throws a low
liner home.

Cole is up the line a foot
or two just like I taught him.
He's crouched low, ready
to deliver punishment to
anyone trying to score.

Through the dust and
crowd, I hear the ump
yelling for Cole to show
him the ball.

I turn to spit tobacco juice
and the roar of our fans
tells me what I already know.

Cashero to Cole

Stover hits a shot through
the night to left field.
Ball hits the tin 300-foot sign
-tink-
and the falls to the ground.

Lopez took 2 false steps on
the pitch and has an acre to cover.
Cashero is sprinting to left
from short for the relay.

Parker was running from
1st on the pitch.
He rounds 3rd as Cashero
catches the throw.

From the dugout I glance
at Cole at home.
He's got a shit eating grin
on his face.

Cashero pivots and throws
a BB that buzzes
as it flies by.

Cole's shit eating grin
turns to laughter as he
tags Parker out 10 feet
up the line from home plate.

188 Pitches

The game was 3 hours
and 37 minutes long.
He was 1 for 3 at the plate with a walk.

We won the game 21-14.
When it was over, they
gave him the MVP.

Somebody's grandmother
was yelling at the tournament
director because her grandson
wasn't the MVP.

He said, *Lady, the other team
used 3 catchers. It's 95 in the
shade and he caught 188 pitches.
He's the MVP just not for passing out.*

His teammates doused him
with water bottles.

I stood off to the side by an
oak tree and let my wife
handle the compliments.
A son needs to learn to live
outside his father's shadow.

That Damn 7 Switch

Phone rings at 2:11 am.
Can you work?
He knew the answer
to that before he called.

Before I could finish
putting my socks on
the trouble shooter called—
*That same damn 7 switch
in Frontenac is off again.*

Need at least 2 tree crews,
a pole and transformer.
In the storm room the clerk
is typing and peppering
me with questions.

Under my breath
I mutter *that damn
7 switch.*

A little after 10 am
a lady in her late
60's shows up
at the building.

Wants to know when
her power will
be back on.

She keeps opening
her freezer every hour
to check the temperature
of the meat.
It keeps getting warmer.

I started to tell her
to quit opening the
door on the freezer
but held my tongue.
*Lady, we've had 3 guys
with chainsaws cutting
trees for the last 4 hours
so we can get in there and
fix that damn 7 switch.*

She's pacified.
I escort her to the door.

She's on the phone
with her 92-year-old mother
who lives with her—
*Mom, they are working
on that damn 7 switch*
is what I hear her say
just as the door clicks shut.

Adam Jameson was born and raised in Pittsburg Kansas. He is a 1995 graduate of Pittsburg State University with a B.A. in History. He has a varied job history but has spent the last 11 years with Evergy as meter reader and now an Estimator. His work has appeared in *Harp, The Little Balkans Review, To the Stars Through Difficulty* and *Ghost Sign* which was named a Kansas Notable Book. He was recently featured on Garrison Keillor's *The Writers Almanac*. His poetry collection *#9 to Sallisaw* was published by *The Little Balkans Press*. He's also spent the last 30 years performing with White Buffalo Poetry and Blues. He lives in rural Pittsburg with his wife Mer, son Cole and a bossy Shi Tzu named Scooter.

www.ingramcontent.com/pod-product-compliance
Lightning Source LLC
Chambersburg PA
CBHW030137100526
44592CB00011B/930